QUOTATIONS ON THE GREAT ONE

QUOTATIONS ON THE GREAT ONE

THE LITTLE BOOK OF WAYNE GRETZKY

Compiled & Annotated by

ALLAN SAFARIK
& DOLORES REIMER

A LITTLE RED BOOK
ARSENAL PULP PRESS

A LITTLE RED BOOK

QUOTATIONS ON THE GREAT ONE
COPYRIGHT © 1992
BY ALLAN SAFARIK AND
DOLORES REIMER
ALL RIGHTS RESERVED
ISBN 0-88978-258-X

CIP DATA: SEE PAGE 6

ARSENAL PULP PRESS
100-1062 HOMER STREET
VANCOUVER, B.C. V6B 2W9

Cover design by Kelly Brooks
Cover illustration by Jim Mullin
Typeset by Vancouver Desktop
Publishing Centre
Printed and bound in Canada
by Webcom

CONTENTS

CANADIAN CATALOGUING
IN PUBLICATION DATA

Main entry under title
Quotations on the Great One
    (A Little red book)
    Includes bibliographical references
and index.
    ISBN 0-88978-258-x

    1. Gretzky, Wayne, 1961-   II. Safarik,
Allan, 1948-   III. Series.
GV848.5.G74Q68 1992   796.962'092
C92-091712-7

INTRODUCTION

What, exactly, might be said to
make the Great great?—is it
deeds, words, demeanour? Or
some mysterious combination of
things? Where does Destiny
come in? Students of the Great
must ponder these questions
every day; of course, it is their
work—while the rest of us slog
on from one day to the next, taking solace in the knowledge that
at least the world seems to in-
clude Greatness in it, whatever
its nature, whenever and wher-
ever it seems to arise, as no doubt
it does from time to time. In the
present epoch, for example, there

is only one among us known everywhere in the vernacular as The Great One, and that person is the occasion of the present volume; or, perhaps we should say, that person's *person* is the mystery underlying the sparkling aggregate of commentary and remark arrayed in these pages.

It must be stated at the outset that The Great One has *confirmed* his greatness in the spiritual arenas of two nations; of this there can be no question, although how much his achievement has contributed to the vacuity of Life in Edmonton is yet to be determined. He might be compared in this instance to Clark Kent, that reticent hero whose departure from Gotham, were it to happen, would surely precipitate among an honest citizenry an existential crisis of unimaginable proportion—especially if he were to marry a movie star and move to Los Angeles. Or worse: what if Clark Kent were to be *sold off* by that older guy who owns *The Metropolis* to the *L.A. Times* and still get the movie star? Don't begin to think about it.

One of the stated purposes of Little Red books is to gather into single volumes the spoken wisdom of the Great, that they might be judged in light of their own words by those who wish to study the "spiritual and sporting models so earnestly sought after by the young, while so easily forgotten by the old." But in the case of The Great One—as it would be in the case of Clark Kent, were he to be real—the public record, while offering a scarce yield of the directly-spoken, has delivered up a rich crop of the what-is-to-be-inferred about the Great One through the speech of those luminaries among us willing to talk out loud about him.

Hence the present work: a study of Greatness that combines the words of The Great One himself with those of his most articulate interlocutors. In these pages, we are confident that students of the Great will find much to chew on—while the rest of us continue to find much to wonder at.

—*S. Osborne,*
Series Editor

ON LIFE
ON THE ROAD
LESS TRAVELLED BY

I have to admit, my childhood was a little different from most. I could skate at two. I was nationally known at six. I was signing autographs at ten. I had a magazine article written about me at eleven and a thirty-minute national television show done on me at fifteen.

—*The Great One*

ON WHAT AN OWNER
OUGHT TO DO IN RESPECT
OF THE GREAT ONE

Whatever you have to do, get him.

—*Glen Sather, advising Peter Pocklington*

ON WHETHER ONE OUGHT
TO LISTEN TO
THE PROGNOSTICATORS

When I was ten they said I'd be washed up at twelve.

—*The Great One*

THAT OLD
FAMILIAR LAMENT

We would have won if we had Wayne Gretzky.

—*Paul Reinhart of the Calgary Flames, after losing to Edmonton in the 1988 finals*

ON THOSE FORMATIVE
EXPERIENCES THAT MAKE ALL
THE DIFFERENCE WHEN YOU'RE
SIX YEARS OLD

The best part was the day I got

my first hockey jock. Major moment.

—*The Great One*

ON FORGETTING THAT REMARK
ABOUT THE PROGNOSTICATORS
In five or six years, fighting will
be totally eliminated from
hockey.

—*The Great One*

FOR EVERY SILVER LINING
AT THE HEART OF IT ALL
He has an extraordinary knack of
catching the goalie off-guard.

—*Mike Liut*

THERE'S ALWAYS THE CLOUD
Wayne Gretzky doesn't play fair.

—*Mike Liut*

ON HOW ALMOST ANYTHING
CAN MAKE ONE'S
FATHER A HERO

My hero as a kid was a man with constant headaches, ulcers and ringing in his ears. He's a funny little guy who stays up drinking coffee every night until 3:00 in the morning even though he's got to be at work at 8:00 the next day. He doesn't have to work if he doesn't want to, yet he never misses a day.

—*The Great One*

ON THE IMPORTANCE
OF REMEMBERING WHAT
HAPPENED TO ABRAHAM
WHEN HE GOT ONE

I'd love to have him as my own son.

—*Peter Pocklington*

ON THE PHIL ESPOSITO FACTOR:
THERE'S FANCY SKATING AND
THEN THERE'S THE OTHER THING

People told me the same thing about Phil Esposito that they tell me about Wayne Gretzky—that he can't skate. I tell them they're absolutely right. He can't skate a lick. All he can do is score goals.

—*Angelo Bumbacco, Team Manager in Sault Ste. Marie, where The Great One played junior hockey*

ON THE INDIANAPOLIS FACTOR
AND SETTING EXPECTATIONS

We had 2,200 season ticket holders when I signed him. A month later sales had skyrocketed all the way up to 2,300. I guess everyone in Indianapolis who wanted to watch hockey had their tickets. The kid didn't make a difference at all.

—*Nelson Skalbania on signing The Great One for the WHA*

EFFECT ON TICKET SALES IN
L.A. QUICKLY APPARENT

Hey, he belongs in L.A. I'm definitely going to get season tickets . . . even if they never win a game it will still be exciting to go now.

—*Magic Johnson*

ON WHAT TO EXPECT INSIDE
JARI KURRI'S HEAD

People said he and I could see the inside of each other's heads when we played, and that's true. Inside Jari's head are twenty-four hour reruns of Richie Cunningham down at Arnold's.

—*The Great One*

ON THE BINARY NATURE OF
WHAT YOU MIGHT BE

If Gretzky's got the puck and you're not nervous, you're insane. —*Western Report*

ON JUST WHOSE BODYGUARD
DAVE SEMENKO ACTUALLY WAS

He was *everybody's* bodyguard.
—*The Great One*

ON WHEN BEING A BODYGUARD
IS NOT REALLY BEING
A BODYGUARD

I wasn't anybody's bodyguard. I was a member of the Edmonton Oilers hockey club. And if anybody on my team needed help, I was there to help him. Gretz fought his battles on the scoreboard, where he was the undisputed heavyweight champion of the world. Me? I just liked to make sure that nobody tried to take any unfair advantage.

—*Dave Semenko*

ON THE BENEFITS OF BEING
A BODYGUARD WHILE
NOT REALLY BEING
A BODYGUARD

And while I never did agree with being thought of as Wayne Gretzky's bodyguard, I'll be the first to admit that it never hurt me at all. I got a lot of name recognition by being associated with Wayne. If I hadn't played on the same team for nine seasons, I wonder how many people would have heard of Dave Semenko.

—*Dave Semenko*

ON THE FANTASY ISLAND EFFECT
OF RIDING THE COATTAILS
OF THE GREAT

Wayne's like having your own

Fantasy Island. It's so much fun to play with him. I had no goals and no assists before getting on his line and then I almost made the record book.　　—Dave Lumley

ON THE ROLE OF
THE PARANORMAL
IN GREAT PLAY

There were nights when you'd have thought they shared the same brain.

—Dave Semenko on The Great One and Jari Kurri

ON THE LAPIDARIAN
PLEASURES OF HAVING
THE GREAT ONE
IN ONE'S POCKET

I'm like a guy showing off a

precious gem in different pawn shops.

—*Glen Sather, Oilers coach*

**OR, TO PUT IT IN
PLAINER TERMS**

The NHL needs something to hang its hat on and Gretzky looks like a hat tree.

—*Gordie Howe*

**WHATEVER YOU SAY, DAD,
NO MATTER HOW CORNY**

Don't get bigheaded on me. No matter how good you are, there's always someone better.

—*Walter Gretzky to his son*

MORE ON THE
BODYGUARD CONTROVERSY

I'm Phyllis Gretzky, and I don't want you hurting Wayne in those corners tonight.

—*The Great One's mother, to Bobby Hull*

ON THE TECHNOLOGICAL
NATURE OF THE SECRET

And there's one of the big secrets to the successful life of Number 99. You can't hit him. He's got built-in radar.

—*Dave Semenko*

AS OPPOSED TO ITS
SUPERNATURAL NATURE

Aside from that one shot [McCreary in the Oilers' second season in the NHL], I never saw Gretz get levelled in nine seasons. He's a magician.

—*Dave Semenko*

ON THE TRUTH THAT EVEN THE GREAT COME UP AGAINST IT

I was on a plane leaving Chicago and the guy sitting next to me said, 'Are you with the Oilers?' 'Why, yes,' I said proudly, 'I am.' 'How many yards did Walter Payton get today?'

—*The Great One*

ON PREFERRING THE SENSIBLE THING; OR THE ROAD MORE TRAVELLED BY

If a guy tells you to get lost, you can smack him in the mouth, which is the sensible thing, or you can walk away. I like to do the sensible thing.

—*Glen Sather, Oilers coach*

ON WHAT IT TAKES

Guys who refuse to lose. Guys who take pride in the team, who won't give up.

—*Glen Sather*

ON GLEN SATHER'S SECRET; OR: SURE, BUT DOES HE CATCH ANY FISH?

He works the way he fishes—not with a tremendous passion, just intensely.

—*Harry Sinden on Glen Sather*

ON WHAT'S REALLY AT
STAKE HERE
It's just amazing how many companies suddenly want you to hold up their product after you've held up the Stanley Cup.

—*The Great One*

WELL, YOU CAN ALWAYS TRY
OIL OF OLAY
My hands were not quite as soft as Wayne's. Then again, he didn't have to bang his on all those helmets.

—*Dave Semenko*

ON WHAT TO EXPECT IF THE FANS
WERE LET IN FOR PRACTICE
He was not a practice player. He had a great time at practice and

when he had to be serious, he would be. Invariably, Gretz would get more criticisms from the nineteen other guys than he'd get if they filled the Coliseum with fans for practice.

—*Dave Semenko*

ON MAKING SPEECHES WHEN
THE TIME IS RIGHT

There was never any doubt who the leader was. He didn't make a habit of giving speeches in the room, but Wayne could tell us what was on his mind when he felt the time was right. And nobody worked harder than Gretz. He led by example.

—*Dave Semenko*

THERE WAS ALWAYS THE
BRIGHT SIDE TO THINK ON

You could sit on the Edmonton bench and know you were in trouble, but also know that sooner or later, Gretz was going to do something about it.

—*Dave Semenko*

ON CARRYING ONE'S FANS
IN ONE'S HEART

'You all right, Wayne? Are you alright?' the trainer kept asking.

'I'm fine,' Wayne whispered. 'How's the crowd taking it?'

LITTLE-KNOWN HAZARD OF
SCORING TOO MANY GOALS

I'm surprised Gretz didn't wear

his arms out raising them after every goal he scored.

—*Dave Semenko*

ON WHO GETS EMBARRASSED BY THE GREAT ONE'S DIVES

You expect more from the best hockey player in the world. All he's doing is embarrassing the officials.

—*Mike Keenan, coach*

AND WHO'S NOT AT ALL EMBARRASSED

I'm not ashamed to admit that I'll dive—pretend to be tripped—if I have to.... If you dive when a guy is hooking you and he gets a penalty, all of a sudden you're

going to get a little breathing
room.   —*The Great One*

ON WHEN DO YOU THINK
WE CAN START TALKING
ABOUT SOMETHING ELSE

I'm convinced the guy is determined to have me talking about
him for the rest of my life. Just
when I think it's safe to go out of
the house, Gretz finds a new
angle.   —*Dave Semenko*

ON THE TOUGHEST
OF THE TOUGH

Everyone knows that hockey is a
tough sport. With the exception
of one or two of us, it's played by
very tough guys. Believe me
when I say that Dave Semenko

was the toughest of the tough. Maybe ever. His reputation for toughness was legendary among the pros. And that was while he was still in junior hockey.

—*The Great One*

BUT OH, THEY WOULD
HAVE LIVED
TO RUE THAT DAY

They should rename the place Gretmonton.

—*unnamed hockey writer*

ON OILERS GOALIE
GRANT (COCOA) FUHR
AND THE ROAD
LESS TRAVELLED BY

If I had to face Cocoa for eighty nights, I'd never have any re-

cords. I'd probably be working
for Bell Canada, like my Dad.

—*The Great One*

LITTLE KNOWN TRUTH ABOUT
WHO DOES ALL THE WORK
WHILE HE MAKES
ALL THE MONEY

He's never in the defensive zone.
When the puck goes in, you lose
sight of him for five seconds. His
wingers and defensemen have to
do all the work for him while he
makes all the money. Pretty soon
they're going to get a little resent-
ful about that.

—*Fred Shero, coach*

AND ALL THAT STUFF
ABOUT WAR AND LOVE:
ON PLAYING FOR THE STANLEY
CUP AGAINST EDMONTON

The formalities and the friendships are over. They're the enemy now, and they expect to be the enemy.

—*The Great One*

ON THE GREAT ONE AND
THE DEMISE OF
THE RECORD BOOK

He's made it obsolete.

—*Lou Nanne*

THE HALITOSTICAL PART
OF THE SECRET

I play best on four hot dogs with mustard and onions. People ask

me what's my secret on ice? Bad
Breath.

—*The Great One*

**ON RISK: WHAT TO THINK WHEN
SIGNING THE GREAT ONE**
If he can't play hockey he's going
to be the most expensive hand-
ball partner I've ever had.

—*Nelson Skalbania, after signing The Great
One to a four-year personal services contract
for $875,000*

**WELL, AT LEAST
THEY GO IN**
Almost every important goal I've
ever scored has been a backhand.

—*The Great One*

OH, THERE'S ALWAYS YE
OF LITTLE FAITH

The way he's playing, his nickname ought to be downgraded to the Good One.

—*Allan Malamud on The Great One's slump of 1989-90*

A GENETIC SOLUTION TO
VIOLENCE IN HOCKEY

We've got to stop breeding animals.   —*The Great One*

PROOF OF THE VIOLENCE
IN HOCKEY

People always ask me, 'Are hockey fights for real?' Yes, they're real. If they weren't I'd get in more of them.

—*The Great One*

ON THE TAUTOLOGICAL
NATURE OF FIGHTING
IN HOCKEY

As I say in my book, I'm not a big backer of fighting. The rules allow fighting to a certain point. To me, that's mayhem. My opinion is that because we're the only team sport that does not eject players immediately for fighting . . . we do not do anything to discourage fighting. My opinion is that because the NHL has done a strong job of enforcing stick penalties, we could eliminate fighting and not have an increase in stick play.

—*The Great One*

OKAY, I THINK WE'RE GETTING IT ALREADY

In order for our game to grow, we should ban fighting.

—*The Great One*

WOULD THAT BE VELVEETA CHEESE, WHIPPED CREAM OR MARBLE CAKE?

What has amazed me most about Wayne Gretzky is his consistency.

—*Jean Beliveau*

ON COUNTING STUPID QUESTIONS

I think I've answered more stupid questions than anybody alive.

—*The Great One*

ON THE UNPATRIOTIC ASPECTS
OF FALLING IN LOVE

Because Wayne Gretzky is marrying an American girl, there is perhaps a sense that The Great One has not been true to his roots.

—*John Robert Colombo*

ON WHAT, IF ANYTHING,
ONE THINKS ABOUT

If anything, I think about how to avoid being special.

—*The Great One*

ON LIVING SPORTS
LEGENDS NOT JUST
FADING AWAY

[Football star Joe] Montana and Gretzky did the thing living sports legends are supposed to do—marry sex symbols.

—*Sports Illustrated*

ON KNOWING WHO
ONE ISN'T

I'm not Mark Messier. I can't turn around and clunk the guy over the head like he does.

—*The Great One*

ON THE DISNEYLAND FACTOR
AND THE DEGRADATION
OF THE SPORT

They're putting a Mickey Mouse operation on the ice. They better start getting some better person-nel. It's ruining hockey.

—*The Great One, after the Oilers beat the New Jersey Devils 13-4*

40

ON THE EFFECTS OF
MAKING REMARKS ABOUT
THE DISNEYLAND FACTOR

You'd have thought I'd criticized Miss Newark or something. The fans went crazy against me.

—*The Great One*

MORE ON WHAT
IT'S ALMOST LIKE

It's almost like he has a photographic mind ... He is totally aware of where everybody is at all times. It's uncanny.

—*Gordie Howe*

WELL, YOU OUGHTTA
KNOW, GORDIE

There's no end to Wayne's brilliance.   —*Gordie Howe*

ENOUGH, GORDIE,
ENOUGH!

He's good and I know because I played with him. If you want to tell me he's the greatest player of all time, I have no argument at all.

—*Gordie Howe*

ON THE PEDAGOGICAL NATURE
OF THE GREAT ONE'S PLAY

He's a great educator for goal-keepers.

—*Western Report*

MORE ON WHAT THAT
SECRET MIGHT BE

He does it with the grey matter between his ears.

—*Bobby Hull*

IF IT DOESN'T PROVE OUT, AFTER ALL, TO BE SUPERNATURAL

No one can do the things he does out there—the back passes, toying with people with the puck right in front of them, and they can't get it from him. It's miraculous.

—*Bobby Hull*

THEN THERE'S INTELLECTUAL SIDE OF IT

Gretzky would dominate in any era. It doesn't make any difference . . . he may every well be the smartest hockey player who ever, ever played the game.

Phil Esposito

AS OPPOSED TO THE
PURELY THEOLOGICAL

No one I have ever seen has been able to think like Wayne Gretzky can on ice. You can hone that talent by studying the game, but believe me it comes from God.

—*Phil Esposito*

PROOF THAT THE LORD WORKS
IN MYSTERIOUS WAYS

Thank God Wayne is the person he is, because he's bigger than the league. He is what hockey is today.

—*Colleen Howe, Gordie's wife*

ON WHEN NOT BEING HUMAN
AND NORMAL IS JUST PART
OF BEING IN SPORTS

I'm not a private person. I like the attention. The only thing is every person is human and normal, but sometimes I can't be. I can't stand in the street and holler at someone and get mad. Sometimes I get that urge, but I can't let it out. It's just part of being in sports.

—*The Great One*

SO WHAT ARE YOU
GETTING AT, RICK?

Gretzky has the look of a bag boy at the local A&P or perhaps the guy working socks and underwear at J.C. Penny.

—*Rick Reilly, sportswriter*

ON MARIO LEMIEUX AND IT
TAKING ONE TO KNOW ONE OR
SOMETHING LIKE THAT

It was just a matter of time before Mario became one of the great players in history.

—*The Great One*

WE THOUGHT HE JUST
SCORED A LOT OF GOALS

What Gretzky has to say about hockey is important and should be listened to.

—*Mario Lemieux*

ON THE HOVERING THREAT:
SURELY EVERY HERO
SHOULD HAVE ONE

Indeed it seems that the high flying hero of the L.A. Kings has

only one important problem in
his life—the hovering threat of
Mario Lemieux.

—*Ric Dolphin, sportswriter*

ON SETTING LIMITS TO WHAT ONE
COULD GO ON DOING AND THEN
NOT GOING THAT FAR

I could go on praising him until
we're all nauseated. I wouldn't
go so far as to say I'd like my sons
to grow up and be like him, but
really, he's okay.

—*Brian Fawcett, intellectual*

ON THE FIRST THING
THEY HAVE TO DO

People say players in the NHL
won't hit me. They all want to hit

me. But they have to catch me
first.

—*The Great One*

ON IT BEING REALLY A MATTER
OF THE BIGGER THEY ARE
AND ALL THAT

Like most great athletes Gretzky
has tremendous pride which,
when wounded, is slow to heal.

—*E.M. Swift, sportswriter*

ON WHAT IT MEANS
TO BE THE
RIGHT STUFF

He has the bigness and superstar
power we like to associate with
Diet Coke.

—*Donald Lenehan, U.S. director of Cola
products*

ON THE ART OF COACHING, ACCORDING TO THE COACH

Sather confirmed he has had a lot more to do with the Oilers' success than simply tapping Gretzky on the shoulder.

—*Jay Greenberg*

WELL, FOR ONE THING, THEY BOTH HAVE A LOT OF TEETH

Even if Gretzky is almost as cute as li'l Danny Quayle, hockey is just so tacky.

—*Frank Derford, sportswriter*

ON RESOLVING THE I-THOU DICHOTOMY

In my book learning to think 'them' instead of 'me' is what makes you a professional, and it's

what makes you a winner. If
there's one thing I'd like to be
remembered for, it's that I tried to
think of 'them' more than 'me.'

—*The Great One*

ON THERE BEING ONE THING
AT LEAST TO SET HIM APART
FROM MARIO LEMIEUX
On sheer ability, Mario is good
enough to win scoring titles with
a broken stick. On pure talent,
he's the best there is. But Wayne
almost never disappoints you.
He comes to work every night.

—*Bobby Orr*

YOU MIGHT WANT TO CHECK
WITH GORDIE ON THAT
Everybody wants to compare

him to Gordie Howe and there is no comparison. I think Gordie Howe was the greatest player who ever played the game.

—*Glenn Hall*

ON NO ONE EVER COMPARING, WHEN YOU HAVE THE PUCK ALL THE TIME

I've looked but I just can't find a weakness in him. They say he can't play defense, but you don't have to when you have the puck all the time. There are great players, but no one can ever compare.

—*Bobby Orr*

ON THE EXISTENTIAL NATURE
OF LIFE AT THE TOP

At 28, his only standard for comparison is himself.

—*Mark Stevenson, reporter*

ON THE INCREMENTAL
INCREASE IN THE AMOUNT OF
EXCITEMENT THAT GOES
WITH WINNING THE
LOU MARSH AWARD

The more often I win it, the more excited I get. Each time you win, it makes it that much harder to win it again. I'm probably more excited about winning this time than any previous time.

—*The Great One*

SURE, BUT WHO'LL MIND THE NET?

I'd trade my whole team for the kid and I'd throw in the farm club too.

—*Harold Ballard, former Maple Leafs owner*

ON THE NEED FOR WIZARDRY IN COACHING

I remember Don Bailey told me a long time ago that I would have to be a wizard to keep this team together because of money. I knew there was no way they would all stick around.

—*Glen Sather*

IF THERE CAN NO PRICE ON GREATNESS, WHAT CAN THERE BE A PRICE ON?

I was offered two million for him, but ten million wouldn't buy him. There's no price on greatness.

—*Peter Pocklington, Oilers owner, before trading The Great One*

OKAY, LET'S GET SOME PERSPECTIVE HERE

Miracles are not going to happen overnight.

—*The Great One, upon his trade to Los Angeles*

ON THE REAL STORY, THE WHOLE STORY AND THE REASON FOR IT BEING A STORY AT ALL

Peter Pocklington is the reason Wayne Gretzky is no longer a Edmonton Oiler. I know the real story, the whole story, and the story of the trade as presented by Peter Pocklington is false.

—*Janet Jones*

BUT YOU ALWAYS KNEW HE'D POP UP AGAIN

I feel like I did when Elvis Presley died.　　　　—*Oilers fan*

WHEN THE BLOOM IS OFF THE ROSE, MUNICIPALLY SPEAKING

Edmonton with Wayne was a glittering city. Edmonton with-

out Wayne is just another city
with a hockey team.

—*Dave Lumley*

ONE WAY OF THINKING ABOUT
WHAT IT ALL HANGS ON

If Gretz brings even one Stanley
Cup to California, it will be the
best deal the Kings ever made.

—*Stan Fischler*

ON BEING LEFT WITH NOTHING
BUT THE NECESSARIES

Hockey is a game of checkers, not
chess pieces, but here is one way
to look at the trade: the Kings got
rooked. To get the Franchise,
they gave up the franchise. Edmonton saw the Kings coming—
as usual. Stripped them clean.

Took everything but their jocks and their pucks. Leave it to L.A.'s hopeless hockey team to make a trade for the greatest player who ever lived and still get taken.

—*Mike Downey, sportswriter*

ON WHAT THE GRETZKY PURCHASE HAD NOTHING TO DO WITH

Obviously, I'm not doing this to make money. I'm a fan.

—*Bruce McNall, Kings owner*

ON WISHFUL THINKING

If people had told me how great I was every day for ten years, I'm sure my ego would be a pretty generous size, too.

—*Peter Pocklington*

ON WHAT THE EDMONTON PRESS CONFERENCE REVEALED OF HIS THESPIAN TALENT

Gretzky has an ego the size of Manhattan. He's a great actor too. I thought he pulled it off beautifully when he showed how upset he was.

—*Peter Pocklington*

ON FINDING NEW LIMITS TO HOW PISSED OFF ONE CAN GET

When I heard that he said I faked the tears, I was the most pissed off I've ever been at a person in my whole life.

—*The Great One*

ON THE PLACE OF BIGNESS
IN WHAT HE WANTS

He wants the big dream. I call L.A. the Land of the Big Trip, and he wants to go where the trips are the biggest.

—*Peter Pocklington*

YOU MEAN, SERIOUSLY OUT
OF POCKET?

Now I know how the guy who was directing *Gone with the Wind* must have felt when he signed Clark Gable to a contract.

—*Bruce McNall, Kings owner, on The Great One's first night as a King*

ON THE PERSONAL TRANSFORMATION TO BE EXPECTED BY MAKING THE MOVE TO LOS ANGELES

Wayne is going to be a golden boy here.

—*Robert Moor, Kings treasurer*

ON ALWAYS DOING THE RIGHT THING

Wayne will do everything possible to help Mr. McNall recoup his losses.

—*Walter Gretzky, The Great One's father*

ON WHEN A THING IS BIGGER THAN BIG

I knew this thing would be big. But I had no idea it would be this big.

—*The Great One*

ON WHAT THE OILERS COACH
DIDN'T ACTUALLY WANT

He didn't want me to make the
deal.

—*The Great One*

ON WHAT ALL FOURTEEN
HUNDRED MILLION OF THEM ARE
WORTH

He's worth every cent.

—*Bruce McNall, Kings owner*

ON THE BEST PLACE TO BE A
BIGGER-THAN-LIFE PERSON
(THE SURFING IS GOOD TOO)

Wayne is bigger than life. What
better place than L.A. for a bigger
than life person.

—*Bruce McNall, Kings owner*

ON THE ABSURDITY OF ANYONE
SERIOUSLY BELIEVING

How can anyone seriously believe that Gretzky's departure from a championship team in Canada for an abysmal team in California will make a difference?

—Frank Derford, sportswriter

BUT JIM, AT LEAST THE BEER
WILL BE CHEAPER, RIGHT?

Who cares why Gretzky is gone? He's gone. He's not our star anymore, he's theirs. If this be free trade, stuff it.

—Jim Taylor, sportswriter

TRY TO LOOK AT IT IN FROM
A LITERARY POINT OF VIEW

Imagine someone in the U.S. offering $15 million and Norman Mailer to McClelland and Stewart for Margaret Atwood.

—*Brian Fawcett*

ON DIVINE INTERVENTION AND
THE RUMPS OF THE CITIZENRY

If the Great One's arrival in the City of Angels does not exactly mark the second coming, it's the closest thing to Divine Intervention that the Kings have seen in their 21 years of trying to put fannies in the seats of the Forum.

—*E.M. Swift, sportswriter*

MAYBE WHAT WE NEED IS
ANOTHER ANALOGY

Wayne Gretzky is a national symbol like the beaver. How can we allow the sale of our national symbols? The Edmonton Oilers without Wayne Gretzky is like *Wheel of Fortune* without Vanna White.

—*Nelson Riis, NDP M.P.*

OR WHAT THEY CALLED A
SOLIPSISM WHEN THEY
CALLED IT ANYTHING

It brings everyone in the league closer to Edmonton and brings L.A. closer to everyone.

—*Harry Sinden, coach*

ON BEING THANKFUL IT WASN'T PITTSBURGH, EH?

Los Angeles. That means I can fly to L.A. and check out the women.

—*Brent Gretzky, The Great One's brother*

WELL, YOU'VE STILL GOT THAT MALL

He was our best reason for living here.

—*Graham Hick, Edmonton Sun columnist*

ON WHAT MIGHT REALLY BE CALLED THE STUFF OF DREAMS

You use other people's money and other people's labour to build your dreams.

—*Peter Pocklington*

A NASTY WAY OF THINKING
ABOUT PETER POCKLINGTION AND
NELSON SKALBANIA

The bearded, slime-scraped Sammy Glick twins of Western Canadian Real Estate.

—Brian Fawcett

ON THE DICHOTOMOUS NATURE
OF CAPITAL AND LABOUR

When an owner makes a business decision, it's just that, a business decision. When a player does the same thing, it's greed.

—The Great One

ON THE ROAD NOW NEVER
TO BE TRAVELLED BY

The louder the ovation got the sadder I became. Life goes on, and you have to forge new relationships but it was very hard on me. I realized what we had and what we could have been.

—*Kevin Lowe, Oilers teammate, on the ovation for The Great One at the All-Star game in Edmonton*

ON THE STRANGE
INVOLUTIONS OF CAUSE
AND EFFECT

What he's doing is obscene. There are going to be records broken, but not the way he's doing it. You hear, well, the game has changed, it's more wide-open since expansion. Then why hasn't anyone else done what Wayne Gretzky is doing? I'll tell

you why—because he's that
much better then the rest of us.

—*Bobby Clarke*

ON BEING BENCHED IN ORDER
TO BE TAUGHT A LESSON

If you want to be a teacher, go to
New Haven [the Kings' minor
league team]. I'm here to win the
Stanley Cup.

—*The Great One, to coach Robbie Ftorek*

ON THE KINGS' EARLY
TROUBLES IN 91-92

I feel like I've been the weak link
of the club.

—*The Great One*

ON BEING THOUGHT CRAZY
BY EVERYONE

To me, to us, Wayne's just another hockey player. He happens to be the best there is, but Wayne comes to practice and works like everybody else. When we say that, everybody thinks we're crazy, but that's the way we see it.

—*Robbie Ftorek, Kings coach*

ON THE QUANTUM NATURE
OF BEING HERE AND THERE
AT THE SAME TIME

As Gordie said, records are made to be broken. I could be sitting over there in 10 or 12 years watching somebody here. I just hope that I remember and cherish this moment from where I am sitting on that side. Because one day it will happen.

—*The Great One on breaking Gordie Howe's scoring record*

ON THE RIGHT PLACE TO BREAK RECORDS

My first choice is to do it in Los Angeles. If I can't, I'd like to do it in Edmonton.

—*The Great One*

ON PREFERENCE AND WHAT'S IMPORTANT AND SOMETHING ABOUT BELIEF AND DRAMA

I would prefer to have him do it here. He lived ten years here. The city meant a lot to him. Hockey is what's important. I can't believe

him. He always does it in such a
dramatic way.

—*Walter Gretzky, The Great One's father*

ON KNOWING WHEN TO
KISS IT GOODBYE

I kissed that record good-bye a
long time ago when Wayne
started getting 200 points a year.

—*Gordie Howe*

ON WHAT TO WEAR
THE NIGHT YOU KISS
IT GOODBYE

If I thought he was going to do it
tonight I would have worn a suit.
The suit will be on in Edmonton.

—*Gordie Howe, the night The Great One
might have broken Howe's scoring record in
Vancouver*

ON KNOWING NO LIMITS
WHEN IT COMES TO
SETTING RECORDS

When it got to be 4-3, if it had
gone in off somebody's rear end I
would have been happy.

—*The Great One*

ON WHAT IT WOULD
HAVE BEEN

I should have had it. I was
bombed. It would have been a
great thrill to score the goal that
broke the record.

—*Bernie Nichols, on assisting on The Great
One's record-breaking goal*

ON THE EITHER-OR NATURE
OF THE QUALITIES THAT
MAKE THE GREAT GREAT

A great man is made up of the qualities that meet or make great occasions.

—*Inscription on Mark Messier's gift to The Great One after breaking Howe's record*

MAYBE ITS TIME TO START
THINKING ABOUT
RACIER UNIFORMS?

When I see our sport is rated 40th in polls in the United States, you start to think—What can we do to improve our sport? How can we make people like us more?

—*The Great One*

ON WHAT OWNERSHIP
OF THE ARGONAUTS FOOTBALL
TEAM TEACHES ONE
ABOUT OWNERSHIP

He's having a tough time coping as an owner. I mean he hates losing. He's very intense. He can't control himself when he sees [the Argos] fumbling or losing. He loses his temper a lot. As a hockey player, he can go out and try to do something about losing. But, as an owner, what are you going to do? You just have to take your losses.

—*Bruce McNall, co-owner with The Great One of the CFL's Toronto Argonauts*

ON THE ANGST
OF OWNERSHIP

But, as an owner, you just watch and get miserable. It's tough to handle, believe me.

—The Great One

ON THE IRONY AT THE HEART
OF CAPITALISM

You lose money like this and it has to affect you. If I keep owning the Argos, I'll have to keep playing hockey.

—The Great One

ON THE FUTILITY OF TRYING TO
HAVE A TALK WITH THE ARGOS

What would I say to them? I mean, I never played football in my life. My father would never let me play because he was worried that my knees might get banged up. So it wouldn't be right for me to talk to them about football.

—*The Great One*

ON THE ROLE OF GOVERNMENT
IN THE FUTURE OF HOCKEY

I'm not a Wall Street man, but I do know that people are more reluctant to spend money on things like sports entertainment when times are tough economically. So we have to rely on the Canadian government. We need the government to turn the Canadian economy around.

—*The Great One*

ON THE FUTILITY OF SPECULATING HOW MUCH MORE OF THE NECESSARY STUFF ARGOS CO-OWNER BRUCE MCNALL MIGHT POUR INTO IT

I don't know how long Bruce will want to hang in there. I don't know how long he'll ride it out. He's put a lot of money in this, believe me. He's poured his heart into it.

—The Great One

ON ROCKET ISMAIL AND WHAT IT MIGHT TAKE TO TEAR HIM AWAY FROM TORONTO

I really don't think Rocket will leave Toronto. I think he likes the

city. Besides, how can he pass up
$4 million a year?

—*The Great One*

ON WHAT NOT JUST
TAGGING ALONG FOR THE RIDE
CAN MEAN

I'm not just tagging along with
Bruce for the ride. Bruce owns 60
percent of the club, but I pay my
own way on every business ven-
ture with him. I buy into busi-
nesses just like he does. So I'm
losing money on the Argos just
like he is, and it's not a pleasant
feeling.

—*The Great One*

ON NOT WORKING
JUST AS HARD, EVEN IF YOU
ARE WORKING HARD

You look out there in practice or in games and you see that the best player in the history of the game is always working hard. You say to yourself—'If he's working hard, how can I not work just as hard?'

—*Bernie Nichols*

ON HOW TO TELL THE
DIFFERENCE BETWEEN
THE GREAT ONE AND ONESELF

I guess you could say there's a little difference between myself and Gretz. He lives in Los Angeles, I live in Edmonton. He has a daughter, I have two sons. Other than that the similarities are rather remarkable.

—*Dave Semenko*

ON WHAT KIDS SHOULD BE DOING INSTEAD OF QUITTING HOCKEY

Kids should be outdoors playing baseball or soccer in the summer. Kids are quitting hockey when they're 16 or 17 because they're tired of it.

—*The Great One*

EVER THOUGHT ABOUT STAND-UP, DAVE?

Wayne had more left wingers [working with him] than Gorbachev.

—*Dave Semenko*

ON RELATIVITY, EXCITEMENT
AND HORSE-RACING

When Golden Pheasant was coming down the stretch and we saw him go to the lead I'd have to say it was just as exciting as anything I've ever won in my life.

—The Great One, on his horse Golden Pheasant winning the Arlington Million

ON THE ROLE OF INSURANCE
COMPANIES IN THE FIGHT
AGAINST AIDS

This is a horrible problem. This is our nuclear war. This is very serious. Sure it affects athletes, but my cousins and kids aren't athletes, and I worry about them. As far as HIV goes, maybe we should be pioneers, be the first sport to step forward, help look for the solution and the cure. I don't think testing takes away from anyone's rights. Each and every person, for their own peace of mind, should be tested. I've had to do it for insurance policies.

—*The Great One*

ON WHAT PLAYERS ALWAYS HOPE FOR OTHER PLAYERS WHO DEMAND 3-YEAR NINE MILLION DOLLAR CONTRACTS

I hope he gets it. The players always hope other players can get as much as they can. If they want him badly enough they'll have to pay him.

—*The Great One, on Eric Lindros*

BUT WHAT ABOUT ANNE MURRAY?
Gretzky is probably the best-known Canadian in the world.

—*Al Strachan*

ON THE WAY
ONE PLAYS
People are wondering how much longer I can go on but I feel good. Barring injury, I'd like to play six more years. The way I play I don't have to rely so much on power and speed.

—*The Great One*

ON GRETZKY AS THE
ELIXIR OF LIFE
Since I've been around the kid, I'm starting to feel young again.

—*Gordie Howe*

ON IT BEING A LOVE
THING DEEP DOWN

I think I do it for the love of the game. I love to play. Everytime I step on the ice, if I don't have a good shift, I'm disappointed in myself. I feel I've let myself down, the team down, and the fans down.

—The Great One

ON BEING A MERE
MORTAL AFTER ALL

Because Gretzky has been super-human in so many ways, we perhaps tend to forget that he is a mere mortal after all.

—Al Strachan

SOURCES

The Globe & Mail

Gretzky (Gretsky/Reilly; Harper-
Collins, 1990)

Inside Hockey

Looking Out for Number One
(Semenko/Tucker;   Stoddart,
1989)

Maclean's

Montreal Gazette

Sports Illustrated

This Magazine

Vancouver Sun

Wayne Gretzky (Hanks; St. Martin's
Press, 1990)

Western Report

INDEX

ALLAN SAFARIK is a poet and free-lance writer, and editor of *Quotations from Chairman Ballard* and co-editor of *Quotations from Chairman Cherry*. He lives in White Rock, B.C.

DOLORES REIMER comments on hockey from Dundurn, Saskatchewan. She is co-editor of *Quotations from Chairman Cherry*.

t is the purpose of LITTLE RED BOOKS to gather the distilled wisdom of great men and women into single volumes so that students of the Great might judge them in light of their own words and the words that others speak of them, to find where they will the spiritual and sporting models so earnestly sought after by the young, while so often forgotten by the old.

LITTLE RED BOOKS
FROM ARSENAL PULP PRESS

*The Little Black and White Book
of Film Noir*

The Little Blue Book of UFOs

*The Little Green Book:
Quotations on the Environment*

*The Little Grey Flannel Book:
Quotations on Men*

*The Little Pink Book:
Quotations on Women*

Quotations for a Nation

Quotations from Chairman Ballard

Quotations from Chairman Cherry

Quotations from Chairman Lamport

Quotations from Chairman Zalm

*Quuotations on Sex and Love
in Canada*